Diet recommendations for TCM - Heart - Yin deficiency

Please check these recommendations always with a TCM nutrition consultant, therapist, doctor or dietician. The recipes and the list of ingredients are supporting also the conventional medical therapy. The calorie disclosures of fresh ingredients (fruit and vegetables) vary according to quality and time of harvest. The contents were checked by a dietician and a nutrition consultant for the Traditional Chinese Medicine (TCM).

Author:
©2017 Josef Miligui
www.ebns.at

AF220121

Source:
The lists are created from the EBNS database for nutritional counseling. The database is used by dietitians, therapists and doctors for advising the patient / client.

Literature:
The specialist literature and the training documents of the German and Austrian dietary and traditional Chinese medicine serve as a knowledge base. We have used the documents as a basis of knowledge, adapted it to our experience and completed them.
http://di-book.com

Title Photo:
©2008 Erika Weixlbaumer

Production and publishing:
BoD – Books on Demand, Norderstedt
ISBN: 9783752862324

Diet recommendations for TCM - Heart - Yin deficiency

1   Treatment strategy

Calm the mind, nourish the heart Yin and Kidney Yin. Hot NO, bitter and salty warm NO (rest LITTLE), neutral and refreshing YES, cold LITTLE.

2   Avoid

Bitter or dehydrating food, coffee, green and black tea, alcohol, lamb, cigarettes, spicy hot spices, very salty food, grilled, roasted, fried, hectic, stress, time pressure, lack of sleep.

3 Breakfast

4 Snack

5 Lunch

6 Afternoon

7 Dinner

8   Any time

9 Recipes

(recommendable) = You can use more.
(little) = You should use less than specified or omit.

9.1 8 treasures of rice

Strengthens kidney and bladder, builds up Qi, strengthens the spleen, repels moisture, reduces internal heat, prevents cancer, builds heart, calms nerves.
Cooking time approx. 1 hour
Calories p. portion: 212
4 portions

Quantity of ingredients
Lily bulbs 1 table spoon / 5g. (recommended)...................................*
Longane 1 table spoon / 5g. (recommended)...................................*
King Solomon's-seal 1 table spoon / 5g. (recommended).................*
Yam root, yam root tuber 1 table spoon / 5g. (recommended)...........*
Coix (seeds) YiYi Ren 1 table spoon / 5g. (yes)...............................*
Rice wild (nature rice) 1 1/2 cups / 240g. (yes) ....metal
Water 8-10 cups / 800g. (yes) .... earth

Cooking instructions:
Each one 1 tbsp: Bai He, Longan, Yu Zhu, Da Zao, Shan Yao, Lian Mi, Yi Yi Ren, Qian Shi Add hot water and soak for about 30 minutes. Then add 1 - 2 cups of rice (normal) and simmer for 1/2 to 1 hour until the rice is very soft. Or: Cook for about 3 hours with the herbs a congee. Then the herbs do not have to be soaked.

9.2 Antipasti

Cools and moves blood, reduces external and internal wind, reduces internal heat, cools heat, reduces mucus, relaxes, distributes, nourishes liver-Yin.
Cooking time approx. 40 min
Calories p. portion: 100
3 portions

Quantity of ingredients

Pepperoni 1 piece / 5g. (recommended).. fire
Lemon juice 1 table spoon / 10g. (recommended) .... wood
Aubergine 1 piece / 300g. (little)... earth
Tomato 4 pieces / 200g. (recommended) .... wood
Zucchini 5/8 oz / 200g. (recommended)..................................... earth
Lemon peel 1/2 piece / 3g. (recommended)................................ fire
Olive oil 1 table spoon / 15g. (yes).. earth
Basil (fresh) 8 leaves / 5g. (recommended).............................. metal
Salt 1 pinch / 0,5g. (recommended)... water
Coriander 1/2 teaspoon / 2g. (little)... metal

Cooking instructions:

Preheat the oven to 250 degrees Celsius and bake the hot peppers until the bowl becomes dark (about 20 minutes). Cover the hot peppers with a clear film and allow to cool. Peel the skin and cut into strips about 2 cm wide. Cut tomatoes in half and spread with oil in slices of aubergine and bake in the oven at 200 degrees golden brown (about 10 minutes) Fry the zucchini slices in the grill pan (without fat).

Mix everything together, mix the marinade of olive oil, salt and lemon peel and pour over the vegetables, sprinkle with coriander. Leave for 1 hour.

9.3   Artichoke soup

Cools heat, nourishes heart, stomach and lungs Yin.
Cooking time approx. 40 min
Calories p. portion: 142
3 portions
Allergens: GLN

Quantity of ingredients

Artichoke 4 pieces / 400g. (yes) .... fire
Butter organic 1 table spoon / 20g. (yes) .... earth
Onion (shallot) 1 piece / 20g. (little) .... metal
Corn flour 1 table spoon / 10g. (recommended)........................ earth
Nutmeg 1 pinch / 0,5g. .... metal
Basic recipe for a vegetable soup 1 cup / 250g. (recommended) .... *
Salt 1 pinch / 0,5g. (recommended)... water
Lemon 1/4 piece / 8g. (little) .... wood
Lemon peel 1/4 piece / g. (recommended).................................. fire

Turmeric (yellow root) 1 pinch / 1g. (recommended) .... *
Sesame paste (Tahini) 1 table spoon / 10g. (recommended) ..... earth
Sesame, white 1 teaspoon / 10g. (recommended) .... earth

Cooking instructions:
Boil the artichokes in 2 liters of water with salt until the outer leaves are light removable. Remove leaves and flower center (fibrous) so that only the soil remains.
Melt the butter, cut the onion into small pieces and steam gently; add some cornmeal, nutmeg; brew with vegetable soup; add salt, a little lemon peel and juice, turmeric and artichoke bottoms, cook gently and puree; Season with Tahin and sprinkle with sesame before serving.

9.4   Beet salad with salad cucumber

Nourishing and slightly refreshing, builds up Qi, strengthens blood and fluids, cools and moisturizes, diuretic, reduces damp heat, regulates Qi.
Cooking time approx. 45 min
Calories p. portion: 264
2 portions
Allergens: GMO

Quantity of ingredients
Red beet 4 pieces / 200g. (recommended) .... earth
Cucumber 1 piece / 250g. (recommended) .... earth
Olive oil 4 table spoons / 40g. (yes) .... earth
Sugar cane sugar 1 pinch / 1g. (yes) .... earth
Pepper (ground) 1 pinch / 0,2g. .... metal
Mustard seeds 1 pinch of powder / 0,2g. (little) .... *
Dill 1/2 teaspoon (chopped) / 2g. (little) .... metal
Onion (spring onion) 2 pieces / 40g. (little) .... metal
Salt 1 pinch / 0,5g. (recommended) .... water
Vinegar (Apple vinegar) 1 dach / 1g. .... wood
Sour cream 15% fat 2 table spoons / 20g. (recommended) .... *
Pepper powder (hot) 1 pinch / 0,3g. (recommended) .... fire

Cooking instructions:
Softly boil beetroot, peel and dice; Peel and dice the cucumber.
Dressing: olive oil, a little whole cane sugar, pepper, mustard powder, dill, finely chopped spring onion, salt, vinegar, a little sour cream and a pinch of rose paprika; stir; mix with the beetroot and let it rest; Add the cucumbers just before serving to keep their light color. Serve with: millet, which together with the salad makes a simple, light meal.

9.5 Bulgur with tomatoes and fresh herbs

Very refreshing, builds up fluids.
Cooking time approx. 30 min
Calories p. portion: 205
1 portions
Allergens: A

Quantity of ingredients
Bulgur (cereals) 1 cup / 120g. (yes)..wood
Tomato 2 pieces / 70g. (recommended) ....wood
Rucola 2 table spoons / 16g. ....fire
Pepper powder (hot) 1 pinch / 2g. (recommended).......................fire
Olive oil 2 table spoons / 20g. (yes)..earth
Pepper (ground) 1 pinch / 0,5g. ....metal
Salt 1 pinch / 1g. (recommended)...water
Basil 4 leaves / 2g. (recommended)..metal
Thyme 1 Twig / 3g. (recommended) ....*
Lemon juice 1/2 piece / 10g. (recommended) ....wood

Cooking instructions:
Put cold water in a pot, sprinkle in Bulgur and simmer. Stir in chopped
tomatoes, fresh herbs like basil, thyme, arugula, a pinch of rose
paprika, lemon juice, a dash of olive oil, a little ground pepper, some
salt.

Variant: add some mozzarella.

Recommendation: ideal morning meal in summer; also suitable as
evening meal, especially for sleep disorders.

9.6 Cherry cereal porridge

Reduces internal heat, moisturizes intestines, relaxes, builds up Qi,
strengthens middle, reduces internal heat, nourishes Yin from heart and
kidney, preserves the fluids, strengthens heart blood.
Cooking time approx. 10 min
Calories p. portion: 219
1 portions
Allergens: AG

Quantity of ingredients

Cherry 1/8 lbs - 2oz / 50g. (little).. earth
Water 3/4 cup - 6 oz / 200g. (yes)... earth
Wheat flakes 1/2 oz / 20g. (yes) ....wood
Banana 1/8 lbs - 2oz / 50g. (little) .... earth
Butter organic 1 table spoon / 10g. (yes) .... earth

Cooking instructions:
Thoroughly wash the cherries, pluck from the stems and core. Drain the cherries from the glass and defrost the frozen ones. Cook the cherries with the water and the flakes in a saucepan over low heat while stirring for about 4 minutes until the cherries are soft. Add the banana and the butter to the porridge, finely grate with the blender.

9.7   Chicken soup with angelica root and buckthorn fruit

Strengthens spleen and nourishes the blood and Yin of the liver, forces Qi and blood, is very warming.
Cooking time approx. 1 1/2 hours
Calories p. portion: 77
3 portions
Allergens: LO

Quantity of ingredients

Basic recipe for a chicken soup 2 cup / 500g. (recommended) ....*
Angelica root 1/8 oz / 5g. (recommended) ....*
Bocksdorn fruits, goji berry dried 1/8 lbs - 2oz / 50g. ....wood

Cooking instructions:
When you cook chicken broth according to basic recipes add angelica root and Bocksdorn fruits in the last 40 minutes.

Ingestion: Drink 2-3 cups of broth daily.

9.8   Clear oxen tail soup with buckthorn fruit

Forces Qi, nourishes the liver blood, good for ocular fibrillation or dry eyes, muscle tension or calf cramps due to blood deficiency.
Cooking time approx. 1-2 hours
Calories p. portion: 217
6 portions
Allergens: O

Quantity of ingredients

Basic recipe for a beef soup 4 cup / 1000g. (recommended)..............*
Beef Oxtail pieces 1,1 lbs / 500g. (recommended)...................... earth
Shiitake, dried 4-5 pieces / 4g. (yes).. earth
Onion white 1 piece / 60g. (little)...metal
Sake 2 table spoons / 20g. ....metal
Ginger fresh 1/2 teaspoon / 2g. (little)..metal
Bocksdorn fruits, goji berry dried 1 table spoon / 8g. .... wood

Cooking instructions:

Soak shiitake mushrooms. Blanch oxtail slices (This removes fat and impurities). Cook in the beef broth for 1-2 hours.
Then add the spring onions, shiitake mushrooms, rice wine, buckthorn fruits and ginger and simmer gently.

9.9 Colorful tuscan bean soup

Cools heat, produces humors, nourishes Yin from heart and kidney, relaxes, builds up Qi, spreads.
Cooking time approx. 2 hours
Calories p. portion: 249
3 portions
Allergens: L

Quantity of ingredients

Kidney beans (red) 1/8 lbs - 2oz / 50g. (recommended).............water
Chickpeas 1 oz / 25g. (yes)..water
Lentils 1 oz / 25g. (yes) ....water
Celery sticks 1 stick / 10g. (recommended)............................... earth
Tomato 2 pieces / 100g. (recommended) ....wood
Fennel seeds ground 1/2 teaspoon / 1g. (recommended) .... earth
Salt 1 pinch / 1g. (recommended)...water
Pepper (ground) 1 pinch / 0,5g. ....metal
Garlic 1 clove / 3g. ....metal
Olive oil 2 table spoons / 50g. (yes)... earth
Water 2 1/4 cups / 500g. (yes)... earth
Basil (fresh) 5-7 leaves / 3g. (recommended) ....metal

Cooking instructions:

Soak legumes, boil and puree. Add vegetables, spices, herbs and oil and cook gently for 2 hours.
Variation: Sweet chestnuts give the dish a special Italian touch.

9.10 Cooling rice dish with grapefruit

Lowers lung Qi, nourishes fluids, dissolves mucus, dries out, passes
downwardly, warms the stomach and spleen, harmonizes the intestine,
forces Qi, reduces moisture, strengthens Qi and Kidney Jing,
moisturizes, relaxes, builds up Qi, spreads.
Cooking time approx. 20 min
Calories p. portion: 234
4 portions
Allergens: GHO

Quantity of ingredients
Rice round grain 1 cup / 120g. (yes) .... metal
Water 5 cups / 600g. (yes) .... earth
Hazelnuts 2 table spoons / 20g. (yes) .... earth
Raisins 2 table spoons / 20g. (recommended) .... earth
Agave nectar 1 table spoon / 10g. (recommended) .... *
Salt 1 pinch / 0,2g. (recommended) .... water
Almond puree 1 table spoon / 10g. (little) .... earth
Grapefruit (Pomelo) 1 piece / 200g. (recommended) .... fire
Butter organic 2 teaspoons / 20g. (yes) .... earth

Cooking instructions:
Preparation on the eve: Pour round grain rice into cold water and cook.
Soak chopped hazelnuts and raisins in some hot water overnight.

In the morning: Stir in a little hot water some agave syrup; add the rice
and heat; add a small pinch of salt, almond paste, chopped grapefruit,
the soaked chopped hazelnuts and raisins and mix; Serve with a small
piece of butter.

9.11 Cous-Cous with date, coco and almondpuree

Forces Yin.
Cooking time approx. 10 min
Calories p. portion: 484
3 portions
Allergens: AHO

Quantity of ingredients
Couscous 1 1/2 cups / 240g. (yes) .... wood
Water 4 cups / 400g. (yes) .... earth
Dates dried 6 pieces / 20g. (recommended) .... earth
Coconut flakes 2 table spoons / 30g. (yes) .... earth

Almond puree 2 table spoons / 20g. (little).................................. earth
Olive oil 2 teaspoons / 20g. (yes)... earth
Apple (sweet) 1 piece grated / 120g. (recommended)................. earth
Vanilla 1 knife tip / 0,2g. (yes).. *

Cooking instructions:
Put couscous and olive oil in a large bowl and pour boiling water over them. Let it swell for 10 minutes. Crush dates and grate apple. Loosen up cous-cous with a fork. Mix in dates, coconut flakes, apple and almond paste.
Sweet to taste. Spices and flavors: vanilla, little chili

Winter variation: pear,
Summer variation: apricot, nectarine

9.12 Cranberry juice

Cools heart heat, nourishes heart blood and Yin.
Cooking time approx. 5 min
Calories p. portion: 43
1 portions

Quantity of ingredients
Cranberries 2 table spoons / 25g. (recommended) .... *
Water 1 cup / 125g. (yes)... earth
Honey 1 table spoon / 10g. (little) .... earth

Cooking instructions:
Mix the cranberries with a little water with the blender to a pulp. Add the remaining water and sweeten with the honey.

9.13 Lettuce with fresh cheese

Forces heart and kidneys Yin.
Cooking time approx. 5 min
Calories p. portion: 802
1 portions
Allergens: AFM

Quantity of ingredients
Leaf salads (bitter) 2 portions / 60g. (recommended)................... fire
Fresh cheese from soya 3/8 lbs - 6oz / 150g. (recommended)...water
Mustard 1 knife tip / 1g. (recommended).................................metal
Lemon juice 1 dash / 3g. (recommended)................................wood

Salt 1 pinch / 1g. (recommended)..water
Pepper (ground) 1 pinch / 0,5g. ....metal
Herbs various 2 teaspoons / 4g. (recommended)...........................*
Black caraway 1 pinch / 1g. (recommended) ....*
Whole grain bread 2 slices / 40g. (recommended)....................wood

Cooking instructions:
Wash lettuce and finely pluck.
Mix 150 ml cream cheese, splashes of mustard, splashes of lemon juice, 1 clove of garlic, chopped fresh herbs, pinch of pepper and crushed black cumin and pour over. Serve with wholemeal bread.

9.14 Millet with egg and butter

Forces blood, Yin and Jing, nourishes Yin, moisturizes in case of internal dryness, forces blood, forces spleen, calms nerves and stomach, strengthens spleen and kidney, diuretic, strengthens Qi and kidney Jing, moisturizes, relaxes, builds up Qi, spreads.
Cooking time approx. 25 min
Calories p. portion: 338
2 portions
Allergens: CG

Quantity of ingredients
Millet 1 cup / 100g. (yes)..earth
Ginger fresh 1/2 teaspoon / 1g. (little)...................................metal
Salt 1 pinch / 0,5g. (recommended)..water
Parsley 2 table spoons / 16g. (recommended).........................wood
Pepper powder (hot) 1 pinch / 1g. (recommended) ....fire
Chicken egg 2 pieces / 100g. (yes)...earth
Butter organic 2 table spoons / 20g. (yes).................................earth
Nutmeg 1 pinch / 0,2g. ....metal
Water 1 1/2 cups / 200g. (yes)..earth

Cooking instructions:
Simmer the millet with the ginger and nutmeg in the water for 5 min. and let it swell for another 30 min.
Cook and peel 1 soft egg per person; pile up the millet on plates and place 1 egg each in a hollow in the millet mountain; Put butterflakes over it. Sprinkle with chopped parsley and the rose paprika.

9.15 Polenta with ratatouille

Strengthens stomach Qi, diuretic, moisturizes, relaxes, builds up Qi, spreads, nourishes liver-Yin, cools heat, produces humors, cools and moves blood, reduces external and internal wind, reduces internal heat.
Cooking time approx. 30 min
Calories p. portion: 226
4 portions
Allergens: G

Quantity of ingredients

Corn Grease (Polenta) 1 cup / 120g. (little).............................. earth
Water 1 1/2 cups / 240g. (yes)... earth
Aubergine 1 piece (large) / 200g. (little) .... earth
Zucchini 2 pieces / 500g. (recommended) .... earth
Onion white 2 pieces / 120g. (little)..metal
Tomato 2 pieces (blended) / 200g. (recommended)...................wood
Olive oil 2 table spoons / 20g. (yes).. earth
Salt 1 pinch / 0,5g. (recommended)..water
Parsley 1 table spoon (chopped) / 8g. (recommended).............. wood
Thyme 1/2 teaspoon / 1g. (recommended) ....*
Onion (spring onion) 2 table spoons (chopped) / 12g. (little) ......metal
Basil 4 leaves / 2g. (recommended)...metal
Parmesan 2 table spoons / 20g. (yes) .... earth

Cooking instructions:

Use double the amount of water to polenta, add salt and oil and heat till it boils. Stir in polenta, stirring constantly. Take off the fire and let it swell for 20 minutes. Meanwhile, cut the onion, fry in a saucepan with hot oil. Add the diced zucchini, tomatoes and melanzani and simmer for about 20 minutes. Add basil, thyme, salt.
Coat baking tray with oil, apply polenta evenly and wait until it gets stronger.
Add the cooked ratatouille to polenta, portion and then put in the oven for a few minutes (possibly with grated parmesan).
Sprinkle with fresh parsley and finely chopped spring onion.
The valuable tip: The Polenta sections are ideal for on the go.

9.16 Porcino mushroom-smoked tofu on toast bread

Nourishes fluids, lets Qi ascend, harmonizes spleen and stomach, moisturizes, relaxes, builds up Qi, spreads.
Cooking time approx. 1 hour
Calories p. portion: 169
2 portions
Allergens: AEMO

Quantity of ingredients
Boletus mushroom 3/8 lbs - 6oz / 150g. (yes) .... earth
Soy Tofu smoked 5/8 oz / 200g. (recommended) .... earth
Olive oil 1/2 teaspoon / 5g. (yes) .... earth
Pickle 1 table spoon / 10g. (recommended) .... wood
Nutmeg 1 pinch / 1g. .... metal
Salt 1 pinch / 1g. (recommended) .... water
Miso paste (soy bean paste) 1/4 cup / 50g. (little) .... water
Lemon peel 1 teaspoon / 2g. (recommended) .... fire
Mustard Dijon 2 teaspoons / 6g. (recommended) .... metal
Pepper (ground) 1 pinch / 0,5g. .... metal
Toast bread (whole grain) 6 slices / 30g. (recommended) .... wood

Cooking instructions:
Use fresh or dried mushrooms. Soak the dried porcini mushrooms in 250 ml of hot water for 1 hour. Drain the mushrooms and cut small. Collect the soaking water and pour it through a fine sieve.
Heat olive oil lightly in a small, coated pan. Add the mushrooms, lightly salt, season with nutmeg and sauté briefly while stirring, add 6 tablespoons of soaking water, simmer gently until the liquid has evaporated.

Mix smoked tofu, the mushrooms, chopped pickle, soy cream, grated lemon peel and Dijon mustard with the cutter or the blender to a smooth spread.
Season the spread with salt and pepper. Serve on the toast bread slices.

9.17 Provencal noodle pan

Nourishes Yin and Jing of heart and kidney, forces blood, reduces internal heat, strengthens spleen and liver, regulates Qi flow, cools heat, diuretic, cools blood, reduces mucus, strengthens spleen Qi, strengthens blood and Qi.
Cooking time approx. 45 min
Calories p. portion: 196
2 portions
Allergens: ACL

Quantity of ingredients
Noodles (whole grain) with egg 5/8 oz / 200g. (recommended) .. wood
Aubergine 1/8 lbs - 2oz / 60g. (little) .... earth
Zucchini 1/8 lbs - 2oz / 60g. (recommended) .... earth
Peppers 1/8 lbs - 2oz / 50g. (little) .... earth
Beef meat 1/8 lbs - 2oz / 50g. (little) .... earth
Garlic 2 pieces / 4g. .... metal
Rapeseed oil 1/8 oz / 5g. (yes) .... earth
Basic recipe for a vegetable soup 1/4 cup / 60g. (recommended) ...... *
Tomato juice 1/3 cup / 75g. (recommended) .... wood
Oregano fresh 1 pinch / 1g. (recommended) .... metal
Rosemary 1 pinch / 1g. (recommended) .... fire
Pepper (ground) 1 pinch / 0,5g. .... metal
Salt 1 pinch / 0,5g. (recommended) .... water

Cooking instructions:
Boil noodles in plenty of salted water, chill and drain.
Wash vegetables, dice aubergine and zucchini.
Core the pepper and cut into cubes of approx. 1 cm.
Braise garlic, minced beef and prepared vegetables in heated oil, pour in vegetable stock and tomato juice and finish cooking.
Add pasta to the sauce.
Heat the whole and season with the spices and salt.

9.18 Quick flakes with compote or jam

Forces Qi, dries out, passes downwardly, strengthens middle heater, moisturizes, relaxes, builds up Qi, spreads, strengthens kidney Qi, essence and brain, forces kidney, warms the middle.
Cooking time approx. 5 min
Calories p. portion: 189
2 portions
Allergens: H

Quantity of ingredients

Quinoa 5-7 table spoons / 50g. (recommended) .... fire
Water 1 cup / 250g. (yes) .... earth
Compote (fruits of the season) 1 cup / 100g. (recommended) .... *
Walnuts 1 table spoon (grated) / 8g. (little) .... earth
Olive oil 1 table spoon / 10g. (yes) .... earth
Honey 2 table spoons / 20g. (little) .... earth
Vanilla 1 pinch / 0,2g. (yes) .... *
Anise (Common Fennel) 1 pinch / 0,2g. (little) .... earth
Cardamom 1 pinch / 0,2g. (recommended) .... *

Cooking instructions:

Put the quinoa flakes in a pan and add water. Boil for 3-5 minutes, pull
from the fire, add nuts and compote. Add a dash of oil. Sweeten as
needed with honey, whole cane sugar or agave syrup.
Spices and aromas: vanilla, anise, fennel or coriander, cardamom, a
little chili.

Winter: apple compote, pear compote, fruit jam.
Summer: plum compote, apricot compote.

9.19 Red berry with whipped cream

Builds up blood.
Cooking time approx. 15 min
Calories p. portion: 124
2 portions
Allergens: G

Quantity of ingredients

Berries of the season 1 1/2 cups / 200g. (recommended) .... wood
Grape juice red 1 cup / 200g. (recommended) .... earth
Sugar molasses 1 table spoon / 10g. (recommended) .... earth
Vanilla 1 pinch / 0,2g. (yes) .... *
Cream (30% fat) 2 table spoons / 20g. (recommended) .... *

Cooking instructions:

Put berries and red fruits (redcurrants, raspberries, strawberries,
blackberries and blueberries) in a saucepan. Add half a glass of
elderberry juice, half a glass of red wine or red grape juice. Add one
tablespoon of sugarcane molasses and a pinch of vanilla. Simmer for a
few minutes and serve with a bit of whipped cream.

9.20 Spelled-grid porridge with berries of the season

Nourishes fluids, moisturises dryness, produces humors, moisturizes intestines, cools inner heat, preserves the fluids, contracts, forces middle, nourishes heart and liver-blood, preserves the fluids, contracts.
Cooking time approx. 15 min
Calories p. portion: 244
2 portions
Allergens: AGH

Quantity of ingredients
Cow's milk (1.5% fat) 1/2 cup / 125g. (yes).....................................*
Water 1/2 cup / 125g. (yes).. earth
Spelled semolina 5 table spoons / 50g. (yes)............................wood
Butter organic 2 teaspoons / 20g. (yes) .... earth
Berries of the season 1/4 lbs - 4oz / 100g. (recommended) .... wood
Honey 1-2 teaspoons / 5g. (little).. earth
Almond 1-2 teaspoons / 5g. (recommended) .... earth
Peppermint 3-4 leaves / 2g. (recommended) ....metal
Cinnamon ground 1 pinch / 0,5g. ....*
Vanilla 1 pinch / 0,2g. (yes)..*
Cocoa 1 pinch / 0,5g. .... fire
Coconut grated 1 table spoon / 10g. (yes)................................ earth

Cooking instructions:
Stir in spelled semolina in cold water and boil slowly over medium heat. After boiling, remove from the heat and let simmer for a few minutes. Depending on the desired consistency, some water may have to be added. Stir in the butter and fine grated nuts in the mash and raspberries. Serve with honey or whole-grain sugar as desired.
Spices and aromas: fresh mint, cinnamon or vanilla, cocoa, coconut

Summer: raspberries, blueberries, strawberries

9.21 Spinach with cottage cheese

Refreshing, builds up fluids, forces Qi, forces spleen, relieves inflammation, moisturizes, relaxes.
Cooking time approx. 10 min
Calories p. portion: 301
1 portions
Allergens: GN

Quantity of ingredients

Sesame oil 1 table spoon / 10g. (yes)....................................... earth
Onion white 1/2 piece / 40g. (little)..metal
Garlic 1/2clove / 1g. ....metal
Spinach 2 handful / 150g. (recommended) ....earth
Pepper (ground) 1 pinch / 0,2g. ....metal
Nutmeg 1 pinch / 0,2g. ....metal
Salt 1 pinch / 0,5g. (recommended)...water
Potato 4 pieces / 200g. (yes)..earth
Sour cream 15% fat 2 table spoons / 20g. (recommended)..............*
Salt 1 pinch / 0,3g. (recommended)...water

Cooking instructions:

Heat in a pot sesame oil, add finely chopped onion, roast glassy; fry a little garlic; stew in strips of spinach for about 3 minutes; add ground pepper, nutmeg, salt, a bit of sour cream as desired or serve the spinach with a large dollop of cottage cheese as an appetizer.
In addition, boil the potatoes in salted water, then peel.

9.22 Strawberry soup with melons

Forces blood, cools blood, preserves the fluids, contracts, moisturizes, spreads, forces heart Yin.
Cooking time approx. 5 min
Calories p. portion: 87
2 portions

Quantity of ingredients

Strawberries 3/4 lbs / 300g. (yes) ....wood
Strawberry Juice 1/3 cup / 70g. (yes)...wood
Lemon peel 1/4 teaspoon / 1g. (recommended)........................... fire
Cantaloupe 5/8 oz / 200g. (recommended)...............................earth

Cooking instructions:

Puree strawberries (fresh or frozen) and strawberry juice with the blender, mix in a little sugar.
Cut melon pulp into small pieces.
Arrange strawberry soup in portions. Put the melon cubes in the sweet soup.

9.23 Summer Salad

Nourishes liver-Yin, cools heat, dissolves mucus, forces Xu-conditions, passes downwardly, brings blood into motion.
Cooking time approx. 10 min
Calories p. portion: 281
1 portions
Allergens: GMNO

Quantity of ingredients
Rucola Handful / 15g. .... fire
Radicchio 1 head / 30g. (yes).. fire
Tomato 15 pieces (diced) / 100g. (recommended)..................... wood
Olive oil 1 table spoon / 10g. (yes)... earth
Olives 2 table spoons / 16g. (yes).. fire
Vinegar Aceto Balsamico 1 table spoon / 10g. (recommended) .wood
Mustard medium hot 2 teaspoons / 5g. (recommended) ....metal
Sesame paste (Tahini) 1 teaspoon / 2g. (recommended).......... earth
Parmesan 2 table spoons / 20g. (yes) .... earth
Salt 1 pinch / 0,5g. (recommended)...water
Pepper (ground) 1 pinch / 0,2g. ....metal
Rosemary 2 teaspoons / 3g. (recommended) .... fire

Cooking instructions:
Wash the salad, pluck it small and arrange it in a bowl.

Sauce: Put the oil, the balsamic vinegar, the mustard and the tahini in a glass with a lid and shake well. Season the dressing with salt and pepper. Mix the salad with the salad dressing and the olives, sprinkle with parmesan and finally with rosemary.

9.24 Sweet-savory barley salad

Cooling, nutritious and moisturizing.
Cooking time approx. 25 min
Calories p. portion: 511
2 portions
Allergens: AGHO

Quantity of ingredients
Water 5/8 oz / 50g. (yes).. earth
Barley 1/4 lbs - 4oz / 100g. (recommended) .... earth
Apple (sour) 2 pieces / 300g. (yes)... wood
Grapes red Handful / 20g. (yes) .... earth

Dates dried 2 table spoons (gutted) / 20g. (recommended)........ earth
Almond 1 table spoon / 10g. (recommended) .... earth
Curry 1 pinch / 0,2g. ....metal
Salt 1 pinch / 0,5g. (recommended)...water
Lemon juice 1 piece / 20g. (recommended) .... wood
Lemon peel 1/4 piece / 2g. (recommended)................................ fire
Cocoa 1 pinch / 0,5g. .... fire
Cream, sweet 30% 1/2 cup / 100g. (yes)..*

Cooking instructions:
Boil the barley in water. Mix cooked barley, 2 sweet chopped apples, a handful of red grapes, about 80 g of pitted dates, about 50 g of chopped almonds, some curry, a pinch of salt, juice of 1 lemon, grated lemon zest, some cocoa.
Leave for 1 hour; Lift 100 ml of whipped cream underneath.

Recommendation: in the summer as a refreshing evening meal.

9.25 Tea from celery sticks

Brings the Liver Qi in motion, cools heat, moisturizes, relaxes, builds up Qi, spreads.
Cooking time approx. 15 min
Calories p. portion: 1
4 portions
Allergens: L

Quantity of ingredients
Celery sticks 2 table spoons (chopped) / 18g. (recommended) .. earth
Water 2 cup / 500g. (yes) .... earth

Cooking instructions:
Heat the water till it boils and put it aside. Add cutted celery and cook for 10 min. to let go. Strain. Sweet to taste with honey.

9.26 Tea from Melissa

Preserves the fluids, contracts, soothes liver fire, stimulates lungs Qi.
Cooking time approx. 10 min
Calories p. portion: 0
4 portions

Quantity of ingredients
Balm 2 teaspoons / 4g. (recommended) .... wood
Water 2 cup / 500g. (yes) .... earth

Cooking instructions:
Heat the water till it boils and put it aside. Add lemon balm and 10 min.
to let go. Sweet to taste with honey. Strain when pouring.

9.27 Tea from rosemary

Dries out, passes downwardly, forces heart, lung and spleen Qi, forces
liver-blood, forces heart-Yin, expels spleen heat / cold moisture,
strengthens spleen and kidney Yang.
Cooking time approx. 15 min
Calories p. portion: 1
4 portions

Quantity of ingredients
Rosemary 2-4 teaspoons / 6g. (recommended) .... fire
Water 2 cup / 500g. (yes) .... earth

Cooking instructions:
Heat the water till it boils and put it aside. Add rosemary and 10 min. to
let go. Strain. Sweet to taste with honey.

9.28 Tea from sage

Distributes mucus, passes downwardly, activates Wei Qi, forces Qi.
Cooking time approx. 15 min
Calories p. portion: 4
4 portions

Quantity of ingredients
Sage 2 teaspoons / 6g. (recommended)...................................... fire
Water 2 cup / 500g. (yes)... earth

Cooking instructions:
Heat the water till it boils and put it aside. Add sage and 10 min. to let go. Strain. Sweet to taste with honey.

9.29 Tea from seaweed

Forces heart and kidneys Yin.
Cooking time approx. 10 min
Calories p. portion: 0
4 portions

Quantity of ingredients
Hijiki 2 teaspoons / 2g. (recommended)....................................water
Water hot 2 cup / 500g. (yes) .... *

Cooking instructions:
Simmer the Hijiki alga with hot water for about 10 minutes. Then drink broth.

9.30 Tea from thyme

Converts mucus, forces lungs and spleen, dries out, passes downwardly.
Cooking time approx. 10 min
Calories p. portion: 0
4 portions

Quantity of ingredients
Thyme 3 table spoons / 6g. (recommended)..................................... *
Water 2 cup water / 500g. (yes)... earth

Cooking instructions:
Heat the water till it boils and put it aside. Add thyme and 10 min. to let go. Strain. Sweet to taste with honey.
Drink 2 to 3 cups daily by mouth

9.31 Vegetable semolina soup

Strengthens spleen and liver, regulates Qi flow, builds up Qi, dries out, passes downwardly, reduces moisture, regulates Qi.
Cooking time approx. 20 min
Calories p. portion: 199
3 portions
Allergens: AEGL

Quantity of ingredients
Basic recipe for a vegetable soup (nutritious) 2 cup / 500g. (recommended)*
Potato 1 piece / 80g. (yes)...earth
Parsnip 1 piece / 180g. (yes)..fire
Carrot 1 piece / 120g. (yes)..earth
Celery root 3/8 lbs - 6oz / 150g. (yes)..earth
Kohlrabi 1/2 piece / 200g. (little) ....earth
Beans (green, fresh) 1/4 lbs / 100g. (recommended) ....water
Wheat semolina 2 table spoons / 24g. (recommended)..............wood
Lovage 1/2 teaspoon / 2g. (yes) ....metal
Butter organic 1 table spoon / 20g. (yes) ....earth
Soy sauce 1 teaspoon / 3g. (little)..water

Cooking instructions:
Worm the prepared vegetable soup; cook the vegetables in the soup softly. Spread some wheatgrass and let it swell. At the end, add lovage-green and a little butter and taste with soy sauce.

9.32 Wheat semolina with olives-herb-sauce and salad

Strengthens spleen and liver, regulates Qi flow, nourishes Yin from heart and kidney, moisturizes, dissolves stagnation, directs upwards.
Cooking time approx. 15 min
Calories p. portion: 245
3 portions
Allergens: ACGL

Quantity of ingredients
Cream, sweet 30% 1/8 lbs - 2oz / 40g. (yes).....................................*
Water 1/3 cup / 65g. (yes) ....earth
Wheat semolina 1/4 lbs - 4oz / 100g. (recommended) ....wood
Chicken egg 1 piece / 60g. (yes) ....earth
Pepper (ground) 1 pinch / 0,5g. ....metal
Lemon peel 1 pinch / 1g. (recommended).....................................fire

Onion white 1 piece / 60g. (little)..metal
Olive oil 1 teaspoon / 2g. (yes).. earth
Chives 1 table spoon / 7g. (little)...metal
Basic recipe for a vegetable soup (nutritious) 2 cups / 500g.
(recommended)*
Lettuce 2 handful / 30g. (yes).. fire
Olive oil 1 teaspoon / 3g. (yes).. earth
Lemon juice 1 teaspoon / 3g. (recommended)...........................wood
Oregano fresh 1 teaspoon / 2g. (recommended).......................metal

Cooking instructions:
Mix cream and water and heat till it boils. Stir in the wheat semolina and
cook to a thick porridge and remove from heat. Whisk the egg and stir
in, season with pepper and grated lemon zest. Form with 2 coffee
spoons, dumplings and leave to stir in the slightly boiling vegetable
stock until the dumplings float up.
Chop the onion and roast it in olive oil in a pan. Pour the semolina
dumplings into the pan and sprinkle with finely chopped chives.
Wash salad and cut into thin strips. Season with olive oil, lemon juice
and oregano.

9.33 Wheatgrassporridge with pink grapefruit

Nourishes fluids, moisturises dryness, lowers lung Qi, nourishes fluids,
nourishes Yin from heart and kidney, moisturizes, preserves the fluids,
contracts.
Cooking time approx. 10 min
Calories p. portion: 398
2 portions
Allergens: AG

Quantity of ingredients
Cow's milk (1.5% fat) 2 cup / 500g. (yes)..*
Wheat semolina 1/4 lbs - 4oz / 100g. (recommended) ....wood
Sugar cane sugar 1/8 lbs - 2oz / 40g. (yes)............................... earth
Grapefruit (Pomelo) 1/2 piece / 120g. (recommended)................. fire
Sugar cane sugar 2 teaspoons / 4g. (yes) .... earth
Cinnamon ground 1 pinch / 0,3g. ....*

Cooking instructions:
Put the milk in a saucepan and heat on the stove. If the milk is warm,
stir in the semolina with a whisk. Add the sugar. Keep it low and wait
until the semolina has absorbed the liquid. Put in a plate and add

chopped crevasses of grapefruit. Sprinkle the porridge with sugar and cinnamon.

10 Effects of food

10.1 Use ingredients: recommendable

Acai powder
Acerola fruit nectar or powder
Agar agar (kelp)
Agave nectar
Agrimony
Almond
Aloe juice
Amaranth
Amaranth Pops
Angelica root
Apple (sweet)
Apple puree
Apricot dried
Apricot jamApricot nectar
Apricots
Apricots juice
Avocado
Baking powder
Balm
Banchatee (green tea)
barberry
Barley
Barley flour
Barley grass powder
Barley grouts
Barley malt
Barley not peeled
Basic recipe for a beef soup
Basic recipe for a beef soup (warming)
Basic recipe for a chicken soup (warming)
Basic recipe for a duck soup
Basic recipe for a fish soup
Basic recipe for a rice soup (Congee)
Basic recipe for a vegetable soup (nutritious)
Basil
Basil (fresh)
Batavia
Bay leaf
Beans (green, fresh)
Bearberry leaf
Beef bone marrow
Beef heart

Beef heart (calf)
Beef kidney
Beef liver
Beef Oxtail pieces
Beef soup meat
Beer (alcohol-free)
Beer (alcohol-reduced)
Berries of the season
Berry juice
Bitter Herb liqueur
Bitter Lemon
Bitter liqueur
Bitter orange peel
Black beans
Black caraway
Black fungus mushroom
Blackberry dried (unripe fruit)
Blackberry jam
Blackberry leaves
Blackthorn (Sloe)
Blue mallow tee
Blueberry dried
Blueberry jam
Blueberry juice
Bocksdorn fruits (Fructus Lycii, Goji, goji berry dried)
Borage oil
Boxhorn clover seeds
Brazil nuts
Bread roll
Bread with carob kernel flour
Breadcrumbs (wheat bread, bread roll)
Brie cheese
Brown ale
Buckbean
Buckwheat
Buckwheat (roasted) Kasha
Buckwheat whole grain
Bush beans
Butter (half fat)
Butter beans white
Calamari
Camembert
Campari

Cantaloupe
Capers in olive oil
Cardamom
Carob flour, St. john's bread
Carp
Celery sticks
Chamomile
Chamomile tea
Channa-Dal
Chard
Chenpi (chinese tangerine bowl)
Cherry (sour)
Cherry compote
Chervil
Chervil dried
Chestnut puree
Chicken Blood
Chicken egg white
Chicken heart
Chickweed
Chinese pearl barley
Chocolate
Chocolate (Diabetic)
Chrysanthemum blossom tea
Clarified butter
Clementine
Coconut fat
Coconut meat
Codfish
Cola drink
Cola drink (low calorie)
Compote (fruits of the season)
Cooking oil
Coriander (fresh)
Corn (fast polenta)
Corn (roasted)Corn flour
Corn germ oil
Corn silk tea
Corn starch
Cottage cheese
Cranberries
Cranberry
Cranberry jam
Cream (30% fat)
Cream 10% coffee cream
Cream sour 10%
Cream sour 20%
Cream sour 30%
Creamer
Créme fraiche cheese
Cress
Crispbread
Crucian
Cucumber

Cucumber (bitter)
Cucumber (spicy cucumber)
Currant jam (black)
Currant jam (red)
Currant juice (black)
Currants (black)
Currants (red)
Curry paste red
Daisy
Dandelion juice
Dashi
Dates dried
Dates red
Deer's Bones
Deer's kidneys
Duck (heart)
Duck (slaughtered)
Ducks egg
Dulse (seaweed)
Dyer's broom herb
Edam cheese
Eel smoked
Elderberries
Emmental cheese
Evening primrose oil
Fennel seeds ground
Fennel tea
Fenugreek (Trigonella foenum-graecum)
Fernet Branca (herbal bitter liqueur)
Feta cheese
Fig
Fig dried
Fish innards
Fish pieces mixed (fresh water)
Fish remains
Fish sauce
Flounder
Flower pollen
Fox nut, gorgon nut, makhana
Fresh cheese from soya
Fresh cheese with herbs
Freshwater crab
Freshwater fish
Fructose (glucose)
Fruit mix juice
Fruit tea
Gail plum
Galangal
Garam Masala powder
Gelatin white
Gelee Royal
Gentian root
Gentian root tea

Ginger oil
Ginkgo fruit
Ginseng
Ginseng liqueur
Ginseng root
Goat and sheep's blood
Goat and sheep's brain
Goat and sheep's liver
Goat and sheep's stomach
Goose blood
Goose fat
Gorgonzola
Gouda cheese
Grape juice red
Grape juice white
Grapefruit (Pomelo)
Grapefruit dried peel
Grapefruit juice
Grapeseed oil
Grass carp
Greengage
Ground
Ground caraway
Guava
Halibut (Flatfish)
Herbal tea mix
Herbs bitter
Herbs of Provence
Herbs various
Herbs wild
Hibiscus
Hibiscus tea
Hijiki
Hokkaido pumpkin
Honey wine (Met)
Hop
Horehound leaves
Horse meat
Jasmine blossoms tee
Jellyfish
Kaki plum
Kalmus
Kidney beans (red)
King Solomon's-seal
Kudzu
Kukicha tea
Ladyfingers
Lamb kidneys
Lamb liver
Lamb's lettuce
Lavender blossoms
Leaf salads (bitter)
Lemon Balm (dried)
Lemon Balm (fresh)

Lemon juice
Lemon peel
Lemongrass
Licorice root tea
Lily bulbs
Lima beans
Lime
Lime blossom tea
Linseed
Linseed (crushed)
Linseed oil
Liver smoothing tea
Longane
Loquate / Japanese medlar
Lotus roots
Lotus seeds
Lovage seeds
Luo Han Guo fruit
Lychee liqueur
Lye roll
Mackerel
Mango juice
Manioc flour
Mare's milk
Martini
Mascarpone cheese
Mayonnaise 50%
Mayonnaise 80%
Mediterranean fish (cod, plaice,
haddock, sea eel, mackerel)
Medlar
Mirabelle plum
Miso
Miso black (fermented)
Mixed Pickles
Mu Erh Mushroom
Muesli
Mulberry fruit
Multi-grain bread (gray bread)
Mung bean sprouting
Mustard
Mustard Dijon
Mustard medium hot
Mustard sweet
Nasturtium (nose-twister or nose-
tweaker)
Nectarine
Nettles
Noodles (wheat) with egg
Noodles (wheat, lasagne) with egg
Noodles (wheat, ribbon noodles) with
egg
Noodles (wheat, spaghetti) with egg
Noodles (whole grain) with egg

Nori, purple seaweed, red algae
Oat flakes roasted
Oat milk
Octopus
Olives green
Orange blossom
Orange dried peel
Orange grated peel
Orange jam
Orange peel
Oregano dried
Oregano fresh
Oyster shell powder
Oysters
Palm oil
Parsley
Parsley root
Passion blossoms tea
Passion fruit
Peanut (roasted)
Peanut butter
Pear
Pearl barley
Pearl barley
Peas, green
Pepper powder (hot)
Peppermint
Peppermint tea
Pepperoni
Pepperoni, red, pitted, halved
Pepperoni, yellow, pitted, halved
Peppers (sweet)
Peppers powder
Perch
Pickle
Pig blood
Pigeon egg
Pinto beans speckled
Plum dried
Plums
Pork Bacon
Pork brain
Pork fat (lard)
Pork ham
Pork ham cooked
Pork ham smoked
Pork kidneys
Pork Lard
Pork lung
Pork marrow bones
Pork meat
Pork sausage (Bratwurst) Pork/beef sausage (smoked)
Pork's intestine

Potato (mealy)
Potato flour
Prickly pear
Processed cheese 12%
processed cheese 30%
Prosecco
Psyllium seed
Pudding powder vanilla
Puff pastry
Pumpernickel (dark bread)
Quinoa
Rabbit (wild)
Rabbit liver
Rabbit meat
Radish horseradish
Radish leaves
Raisins
Raspberry jam
Raspberry leaf tea
Red beet
Red berry (without sugar)
Ribworttea
Rice (Gaoliang / Sorghum)
Rice long grain rice
Rice mash
Rice starch
Rice sticky
Rose blossom tea
Rose hip
Rose leaf tea
Rosefish
Rosemary
Rum
Rusk
Rye wholemeal bread
Safflower (Dyer's thistle / Hong Hua)
Sage
Salt
Salt (herbal)Savory
Savoy cabbage / kale
Sea buckthorn
Sea cucumber
Sesame oil roasted
Sesame paste (Tahini)
Sesame, black
Sesame, white
Sheep's milk
Sheep's milk yoghurt
Sherry (whine)
Shrimps
Skim milk powder
Slug
Sour cream 15% fat
Sour milk

Sourdough
Soy flour
Soy noodles
Soy Tofu
Soy Tofu smoked
Soya Cuisine (soy cream)
Soybeans
Soybeans, blacks, fermented
Spelled flakes
Spinach
Spurdog (spiny dogfish, Schillerlocken)
St. Benedict's thistle, blessed thistle,
holy thistle, spotted thistle
Stevia (candyleaf, sweetleaf)
Strawberry jam
Sugar - icing sugar
Sugar molasses
Sugar palm sugar
Sugar substitute (sweetener)
Sunflower seeds
Supplementary nutrition
Tabasco
Tea mixture uric acid lowering
Thistle oil
Thyme
Thyme dried
Toast bread (whole grain)
Tomato
Tomato dried
Tomato juice
Tomato paste
Tomato puree
Tonic Water
Trout
Trout (smoked)
Truffle
Tsampa (roasted barley flour)
Turkey ham
Turmeric (yellow root)Turnip
Turnips
Umeboshi paste
Valerian

Vanilla pod
Vanilla sugar natural
Vinegar (Red wine vinegar)
Vinegar Aceto Balsamico
Vinegar Aceto Balsamico white
Walnut oil
Watermelon
Wax gourd
Wheat flatbread/pita bread
Wheat flour whole grain
Wheat germ oil
Wheat semolina
Wheat semolina for children
Wheat/Rye/Gray-black bread with yeast
Wheatgrass juice
Wheatgrass powder
Whey
White bread (baguette)
White bread (pretzel sticks)
White bread (roll)
White bread (wheat bread)
White breadcrumbs
White cabbage
White dumpling bread (wheat bread cut
into chunks)
Whitefish
Whole grain bread
Wholemeal flour
Wild garlic (garlic spinach)
Wild herbs
Wild strawberries
Wormwood
Wormwood herb
Yam root, yam root tuber
Yarrow
Yeast
Yew nut
Yoghurt vanilla
Yogurt (natural, 1.5% fat)
Yogurt (natural, 3.5% fat)
Zucchini

10.2 Use ingredients: yes

Adzuki beans
Apple (sour)
Apple juice (natural cloudy)
Arrowroot
Artichoke
Beef lungs (calf)
Beef meat (calf)
Beer (Pils)
Beer (Top-fermented German dark

beer)
Blackberry´s
Black-eyed peas
Blueberry
Boletus mushroom
Broad beans (thick beans)
Broccoli
Brussels sprouts
Bulgur (cereals)

Butter organic
Buttermilk
Carrot
Carrot (Early Carrot)
Carrot juice without sugar
Cashews
Cauliflower
Celery root
Champignon
Chanterelle
Chicken egg
Chicken yolk
Chickpeas
Chicory
Chinese cabbage
Chlorella (fresh water)
Clementines
Coconut flakes
Coconut grated
Coix (seeds) YiYi Ren
Corn
Couscous
Cow's milk (1.5% fat)
Cow's milk (whole milk 3.5% fat)
Cranberry
Cranberry juice
Cream, sweet 30%
Curd cheese 20%
Curd cheese 40%
Currant (black)
Currant (red)
Currant (white)
Elderberry blossom tee
Endive salad
Fresh cheese
Goose
Goose parts
Gooseberry
Gourd
Grapes red
Grapes white
Hawthorn
Hazelnuts
Iceberg lettuce
Kefir
Kombu seaweed (Saccharina japonica)
Lentils
Lentils black
Lentils red
Lentils yellow
Lettuce
Lovage
Lychee
Lychee in Preserved

Mallow (Malva sylvestris) blossom tea
Malt
Maple syrup
Margarine
Margarine (diet)
Millet
Millet flakes
Morel (black, dried)
Morel, dried
Mozzarella
Mung bean
Octopus
Olive oil
Olives
Parmesan
Parsnip
Peanut oil
Peanuts
Pear juice
Peas
Pigeon
Pine nuts
Pistachios
Pork heart
Pork knuckle
Pork skin
Potato
Pumpkin seeds
Quail
Quail egg
Quince
Rabbit
Radicchio
Radish black
Rapeseed oil
Raspberry
Raspberry dried (immature)
Red cabbage
Reishi mushroom
Rice (fragrance)
Rice Basmati
Rice malt
Rice noodles
Rice red
Rice round grain
Rice sweet
Rice wild (nature rice)
Romaine lettuce / lettuce salad
Rye
Rye flour
Saffron
Salmon
Salsify
Sauerkraut (cutted cabbage fermented)

Sesame oil
Shiitake, dried
Sour cherries
Soybean milk
Soybeans, black
Soybeans, yellow
Spelled (Dark) bread
Spelled grain
Spelled semolina
Spelled wholemeal flour
Strawberries
Strawberry Juice
Sugar candy white
Sugar cane sugar
Sugar fructose - fruit sugar
Sugar glucose - grapes sugar
Sugar Milk Sugar

Sunflower oil
Sweet potato
Tangerine
Tarragon (Estragon)
Topinambur
Vanilla
Vanilla powder
Vegetable juice
Wakame
Water
Water hot
Wheat
Wheat bulgur
Wheat flakes
Wheat flour
White beans

10.3 Use ingredients: little

Almond marzipan
Almond milk
Almond puree
Anise (Common Fennel)
Apricot
Asparagus (green or white)
Aubergine
Bamboo shoots
Banana
Banana (cooking banana)
Bean oil
Beef fillet
Beef meat
Beef meatbones
Beef stomach
Borage
Burdock root tea
Carambola (Star fruit)
Caviar
Cherry
Cherry juice
Chestnuts
Chives
Clove
Coconut milk
Coriander
Corn Grease (Polenta)
Crab
Cumin (Caraway seed)
Dandelion (young plants)
Dandelionroots tea
Deer meat
Dill

Fennel
French beans
Ginger fresh
Goose egg
Green spelt
Honey
Kiwi
Kohlrabi
Kumquats
Lamb's lettuce
Leek
Lemon
Mango
Marjoram
Miso paste (soy bean paste)
Mullet
Mussels
Mustard seeds
Oat
Oat flakes (whole grain)Oat flour
Oat fusion (baby food)
Oat meal
Okra
Onion (shallot)
Onion (spring onion)
Onion read
Onion white
Orange
Orange juice
Oyster mushroom
Papaya
Peaches
Peaches (canned)

Peppers
Pheasant
Pineapple
Pineapple (from a can)
Pineapple juice without sugar
Plum
Pomegranate
Pork stomach
Pumpkin
Pumpkin seed oil
Rhubarb
Rice (whole grain)
Rice black
Rice flour
Rice variety any
Rose hip tea

Sago (cereals)
Seacrab
Sorrel
Sour milk cheese 20%
Soy sauce
Soybean oil
Star anise
Sugar brown
Sugar white
Umeboshi plums (Japanese apricots)
Walnuts
Wheat beer
Wheat bran
Wild boar meat
Yarrow tea

10.4 Do not use contra-acting foods

x Anchovy / Sardine
Black tea
Cereal coffee
Chicken liver
Chicken meat
Chicken stomach
Chili (pod or ground)
Cinnamon ground
Cinnamon sticks
Cocoa
Cod
Coffee
Curcuma
Curry
Deer meat
Eel
Feta cheese
Garlic
Ginger powder
Goat
Goat and sheep's milk
Goat cheese
Green tea
Herring
Hyssop
Juniper berry
Lamb bones
Lamb meat
Lamb shoulder
Lobster

Mineral water
Mold cheese
Mulled Wine Spice
Mutton
Mutton
Nutmeg
Pepper (ground)
Pepper Cayenne
Pepper white (ground)
Peppercorns
Peppers (rose peppers)
Pimento
Plaice
Poppy
Pork liver
Radish
Radish (white, green, purple-red)
Red wine
Rucola
Sake
Shark
Shrimp
Spiny lobsters
Spirit
Tuna
Turkey breast meat
Vinegar (Apple vinegar)
Walnuts roasted
White wine
Yogi tea

11 Herbs and their effects

11.1 Basil

thermal effect: warm
taste: spicy, bitter
Dries out, leads down. Tonifies Yang and Qi, dissolves mucus-cold, eliminates wind-cold.
It has a beneficial effect on flatulence and nausea, relaxing and soothing.
Good to fight emphysema, bronchitis, whooping cough, high blood pressure, headache, mouth odor, warts, hiccup, gout, migraine.

11.2 Dill

thermal effect: warm
taste: spicy
Moves qi, triggers stagnation, heads up.
The medicinal and spice herb has an antispasmodic effect and stimulates gastric juice production. Good to fight flatulence. Antispasmodic for gastrointestinal discomfort.

11.3 Coriander

thermal effect: warm
taste: spicy
Driving sweat, reducing wind, draining moisture, tonifying and regulating qi, eliminating wind-cold.
The essential oils are appetizing, digestive, cramping and soothing in stomach and intestinal disorders.

11.4 Herbs various

Stimulates appetite. Effect different.
Appetizing, lots of trace elements and vitamins.

11.5 Chives

thermal effect: warm
taste: spicy
Directs upward. Tonifies blood, kidney Yang and Qi. Dissolves moisture.
Bactericide, prevents cancer, strengthens gastric juice production, promotes digestion and blood circulation, promotes growth, triggers stagnation.

11.6 Lovage

thermal effect: warm
taste: spicy, bitter
Reduces inner wind and moisture, dissolves stagnation, directs upward, warms Yang, regulates and moves Qi, warms inside, dissolves mucus-cold, eliminates wind-cold.
Stimulates digestion, reduces pain. Extracts of the root are used to flush out urinary tract infections and prevent kidney gravel.

11.7 Lily bulbs

thermal effect: cool
taste: sweet, bitter
Tonifies Yin, soothes Shen / Spirit. Moisturizes the lungs, clears heat and stops coughing.
Calms nerves, good to fight scaly skin. The onions and the petals are added to ointments in the Orient, which can heal muscles and tendons. White lily (astringent).

11.8 Balm

thermal effect: warm
taste: bitter
Keep the fluids, pulls together, soothe lever fire, soothe Shen, stimulate Lung Qi. Regulates qi, eliminates heat caused by yin deficiency.
Soothing effect, Good for insomnia, restlessness and upset stomach, Allergies, Asthma, Migraine, Flatulence, Headache, Rheumatism and mental tension. To strengthen after cold and infectious diseases.

11.9 Oregano fresh

thermal effect: warm
taste: bitter
Dries out, directs down, regulates and moves Qi, eliminates wind-cold, soothes Shen / Spirit, suppresses inner wind, warms inside, eliminates wind-cold / heat-wetness, moves blood, dissolves slime-cold.
It has an anti-digestive, calming and nerve-strengthening effect, helps to fight cramping stomach and intestinal disorders. The ingredient Carvacrol has an anti-inflammatory effect.

11.10   Parsley

thermal effect: warm
taste: bitter
Nourishes blood and liver, harmonizes liver and spleen, strengthens eyesight, preserves juices, contracts. Dissolves moisture and warms Yang.
Stimulates liver function, detoxifies. Forces urinating. Relieves flatulence. Digestive and menstrual stimulating, birth-accelerating, memory-enhancing, blood-purifying, skin-smoothing.

11.11   Peppermint

thermal effect: cool
taste: spicy, bitter
Cools heat, expels mucus, dissipates wind-cold and wind-heat, moves stomach qi, releases congestion, tonifies, regulates and moves qi. Relaxes, frees the lungs and the nose (inhale), regulates the cycle. Stimulates bile flow and bile production, antispasmodic in gastrointestinal disorders, antimicrobial and antiviral.

11.12   Rosemary

thermal effect: warm
taste: bitter
Dries out, leads down. Strengthens the heart, lungs and spleen qi, strengthens liver blood. Strengthens heart-Yin. Expels spleen heat / cold moisture. Strengthens spleen and kidney yang.
Promotes digestion, relieves bloating, strengthens lung, spleen and kidney. Affects the circulation and nerves. Appetizing. Baths help to fight circulatory disorders as well as with gout and rheumatism.

11.13   Sage

thermal effect: neutral
taste: bitter, spicy
Expels slime, guides down, strengthens Qi, eliminates Wind-Heat, eliminate heat induced by Yin deficiency.
Good to fight yeast infections. The leaves have a digestive effect and are used in greasy foods. Antiperspirant effect. Helps to relieve coughing attacks. Dries out.

11.14 Black caraway

thermal effect: warm
taste: spicy, sweet
Dissolve / transform moisture, tonifyes Yang and Qi, moves blood, suppresses inner wind.
Detoxifying, immunoregulatory. In addition, the oil should stimulate the formation of bone marrow cells and generally protect body cells from viruses.

11.15 King Solomon's-seal

thermal effect: neutral
taste: sweet, bitter
Tonifies Yin and Qi, astringent, tonifies blood, eliminates wind-cold / heat-wetness.
Used to repair wounds or damaged tissue. Good to fight dry cough, earlier also tuberculosis and dysentery, as well as diarrhea and hemorrhoids.

11.16 Yam root, yam root tuber

thermal effect: neutral
taste: sweet
Tonifies Yin, Yang and Qi, reduces inner wind, dissolves wetness, warms Yang.
Solves cramps (in the gastrointestinal tract). Digestive through increased bile production. Anti-inflammatory in rheumatic diseases.
Mucolytic agent for coughing. Relief of menopausal symptoms.

12 Basics of Nutrition

The basic principles of nutrition described herein are general recommendations. They are not aimed at a specific form of therapy. Recommendations concerning a therapy have priority.

12.1 Nutrition

Regular meals in a relaxed atmosphere. A warm breakfast is considered a good start into the day.
The main meals ought to be taken for lunch – supper in the early evening. Pay attention to feeling hungry or sated: don't eat too much nor remain hungry is the rule
Prepare the meals freshly from natural, regional products. Frozen, heat-conserved, industrially prepared or foodstuffs cooked in the microwave oven are rejected.
Choice of foodstuffs according to the season: more cooling food in summer, more warming food in winter.
Eat cooked food at least twice a day. Food and drinks ought to be lukewarm, never ice-cold or hot.
Raw vegetables, briefly cooked vegetables, freshly squeezed juices and mineral water are not recommended. Milk and dairy products are only included in the diet if they don't cause problems. Don't use therapeutic recipes over a longer period without consulting your doctor or therapist.

Varied food
Enjoy the diversity of foodstuffs. Characteristics of a balanced nutrition are variety, suitable combination and a balanced quantity of rich and low energy foodstuffs (on one hand avoiding undersupply with essential nutrients and on the other hand to take to many undesirable substances).

A lot of Cereal Products - and Potatoes
Bread, pasta, rice, cereal flakes (best wholemeal) as well as potatoes contain almost no fat, but many vitamins, mineral nutrients, trace elements, roughage and secondary plant substances. These foodstuffs ought to be taken with low-fat side dishes.

Vegetables and Fruit – „Take Five" every day ... 5 portions of vegetables and fruit a day, as fresh as possible, briefly cooked, or maybe one portion as a juice – ideal as a side dish to every meal as well as snack between meals: Thus a lot of vitamins, mineral nutrients as well as roughage and secondary plant substances

Daily milk and dairy products
Milk and Dairy Products every Day, once or twice per Week Fish; meat, sausages as well as eggs moderately. These foodstuffs contain valuable nutrients like calcium in the milk, iodine selenium and omega-3 fat acids in saltwater fish. Meat is favorable due to its high content of disposable iron and the vitamins B1, B6 and B12. Quantities of 300 – 600 g meat and sausage per week are sufficient. Prefer low-fat products, especially in meat- and dairy products.

Low-fat and fatty Foodstuffs
Fat supplies us with essential fat acids and fatty foodstuffs contain also fat-soluble vitamins. Fat is high in energy; therefore much fat in the food may cause overweight, possibly also cancer. Too many saturated fat acids may further a tendency for cardio-vascular diseases in the long term. Prefer vegetable oils and fats (e.g. rapeseed-, olive-, soya-oils and solid fats produced therefrom). Beware of invisible fat in meat- and dairy products, pastry and sweets as well as in fast-food and convenience foods. 70 – 90 g fat per day is sufficient.

Moderately Sugar and Salt
Take sugar and foods/drinks containing various kinds of sugar (e.g. glucose syrup) only occasionally. Use herbs and spices as well as a little salt creatively. Prefer salt containing iodine.

Plenty of Liquids
Water is absolutely essential. Drink 1-2 l liquids every day. Prefer water (with or without gas) and other low-calorie drinks. Alcoholic drinks should not be taken.

Tasty Dishes, carefully cooked
Cook the meals with as low temperatures and as short as possible, using little water and fat – this preserves the original taste, keeps the nutrients intact and prevents the production of harmful compounds.

Take time and enjoy the food
Take your Time and enjoy your Food
Eating consciously helps to eat right. The eye enjoys food, too. It's fun, invites to enjoy varied dishes and stimulates the feeling of satiety.

Watch your Weight and stay in Motion
A balanced diet and a lot of exercise and sport (30 – 60 min/day) are a healthy combination. The right weight furthers well-being and health. Thermals, directional effectiveness, digestive power

There are various criteria for judging the effectiveness of herbs and foodstuffs.

The use of certain herbs and ingredients is based on observations of the effects on the body which these foodstuffs, herbs and spices show after having eaten them. The medical science has developed following system: Every ingredient or herb has a directional effectiveness. Furthermore, there are herbs which have a special effect on certain organs.

The basic condition for a healthy metabolism is to obtain sufficient energy from food and that the digestive process doesn't use too much energy. An easily digestible meal makes content and sated, doesn't cause flatulence and fatigue after the meal. The perfect spices increase the healthiness of our meals. Very often, just small doses of herbs and spices will suffice. They are not used to make us sated, but to help our digestive organs to digest the food.

12.2 Recipes

The recipes list the ingredients to be used and the cooking instructions show how the dish is prepared. The list of ingredients shows the concerned quantities as well as the relevance for the therapy. If you find „less than mentioned", try to comply or find an alternative from the „list of recommended foodstuffs". Mostly it shall result just in a small change of taste when you simply avoid this ingredient.

Mild cooking methods: boiling, stewing, poaching, steaming
Strong cooking methods: barbecuing, roasting, frying, smoking
Balanced cooking methods: deep-frying, baking brick
Deep-freezing and warming in the microwave oven should be avoided (denaturalization).

12.3 Foodstuffs

Foodstuffs have an effect on body and soul like medicinal herbs, only a very much milder one. Dietary advice is mainly based on regional foodstuffs. The knowledge about the effects of each foodstuff and the knowledge, when which foodstuff shall be used, is based on the orthodox school of medicine. Use ecologic-organic products, if possible. As everything should be cooked for a long time due to a better digestability and very rarely eaten raw, the food agrees with everyone.

The classification of the foodstuffs according to their effect on the body is the basis in order to achieve a harmonious status of health.

Dietary advisors do not recommend certain foodstuffs for everyone. The individual diet is tailor-made for the individual constitution.

Buy only fresh and ripe fruit and vegetables. You ought to leave unripe fruit and vegetables and such with brown spots and wilted leaves behind in the market. In this case take deep-frozen goods (never ready-to-serve dishes!). Fruit and vegetables are deep-frozen immediately after harvesting and often contain more vitamins and minerals than the goods from the vegetable shelf. Whereas conserved or tinned goods contain very much less biological substances. Also, salt, sugar and others are mostly added to the latter. Never leave the foodstuffs in the water after washing them to avoid that many vital substances get drowned. Clean salads, fruit and vegetables immediately before serving.

Please make sure of the hygienic processing of foodstuffs. Clean your salads, fruit and vegetables carefully. When cooking with meat, prepare all ingredients first and then process the meat products. Clean the worktop and tools very carefully. Wooden surfaces ought to be treated with a mild disinfectant regularly in order to reduce germination.
Store fruit and vegetables separately, if possible. Harvested fruit and vegetables are still alive and emit e.g. ethylene gas, which makes other products ripen and age faster. Keep meat and fish in the closed packaging or store them in the fridge in closed containers.

12.4 Herbs

There are some basic rules for storing medicinal herbs. On principle, herbs must be protected from direct sunlight, humidity and heat.

Containers for the storage of herbs may be glasses, ceramic jars and even plastic containers. However, plastic is a rather unsuitable material and should only be a short-term solution. In case of glass containers, use a dark material.

Medicinal herbs cannot be kept for any long period. The shelf life of herbs is limited. However, it can be prolonged with suitable storage. The place should be dark, rather cool and absolutely dry. A wooden medicine cabinet, placed not directly next to a source of heat, would be ideal. Never buy large quantities of herbs so as not to have to throw them away. Label the container with the name of the herb and the date of harvesting or processing.

13 Other dietic-books

The following syndromes of dietetics, TCM or for a therapy supplement for cancer are available.

Dietetics

E001. Nutrition of the infant - baby food
E002. Nutrition during lactation
E003. Nutrition in old age
E004. Nutrition of children and adolescents
E005. Nutrition of athletes
E006. Light weight
E007. Pregnancy
E008. Full food

Protein and electrolyte - kidneys
E009. (hemodialysis) dialysis treatment
E010. Acute renal failure
E011. Chronic renal insufficiency
E012. Nephrotic syndrome
E013. Kidney stones (nephrolithiasis)

Gastrointestinal tract - pancreas
E014. Acute pancreatitis (inflammation of the pancreas)
E015. Chronic pancreatitis (inflammation of the pancreas)

Gastrointestinal tract - small intestine and large intestine
E016. Acute obstipation (constipation)
E017. Chronic obstipation (constipation)
E018. Colon irritabile
E019. Diverticulitis
E020. Acquired lactose intolerance (lactose malabsorption)
E021. Fructose malabsorption
E022. Glutensensitive enteropathy (celiac disease)
E023. Colectomy
E024. Short Bowel Syndrome

Gastrointestinal tract - liver, gallbladder, bile ducts
E025. Acute and chronic hepatitis (inflammation of the liver)
E026. Cholelithiasis (bile stones)
E027. fatty liver
E028. cirrhosis

Gastrointestinal tract - Stomach and duodenal intestine
E029. Acute gastritis
E030. Chronic gastritis
E031. Stomach bleeding
E032. Ulcus ventriculi and duodenal ulcer
E033. Condition after gastric surgery

Gastrointestinal tract - oral cavity and esophagus
E034. Stomatitis
E035. Esophageal carcinoma (esophageal cancer)
E036. Refluosophagitis (heartburn)

Special diseases
E037. Phenylketonuria (PKU)
E038. Rheumatic joint diseases

Metabolism
E039. Obesity (overweight)
E040. Diabetes mellitus
E041. Eating disorders (underweight)

Fat metabolism
E042. Hypercholesterolaemia (increased cholesterol level)
E043. Hepatic Encephalopathy

Heart and circulation
E044. Arteriosclerosis (arterial calcification)
E045. Heart insufficiency
E046. Hypertension
E047. Hyperuricaemia and gout

Changed nutrient requirements
E048. In case of fever
E049. For malignant diseases
E050. After burns
E051. Radiation and chemotherapy

CANCER
E100. Pancreatic cancer
E101. Bladder cancer
E102. Blood cancer (leukemia)
E103. Breast cancer
E104. Colorectal cancer
E105. Gastric cancer
E106. Kidney cancer
E107. Esophageal cancer

TCM
E200. Bladder - moisture heat in the bladder
E201. Bladder - moisture and cold in the bladder
E202. Bladder - emptiness and cold in the bladder
E203. Large intestine - external cold affects the large intestine
E204. Large intestine - moisture heat in the large intestine
E205. Large intestine - heat blocks the intestine II acute
E206. Large intestine - dryness of the colon
E207. Large intestine - Yang deficiency (cold)
E208. Heart - Blood insufficiency
E209. Heart - Blood stagnation
E210. Heart - Fire
E211. Heart - Hot mucus clogs the heart pores

E212. Heart - Cold mucus clogs the heart pores
E213. Heart - Qi deficiency
E214. Heart - Yang deficiency
E215. Heart - Yin deficiency
E216. Liver - Ascending Liver Yang
E217. Liver - Blood deficiency
E218. Liver - Blood stagnation
E219. Liver - Moisture heat in liver and gall bladder
E220. Liver - Fire
E221. Liver - Gall bladder Qi-Empty
E222. Liver - Cold in the liver meridian
E223. Liver - Qi stagnation
E224. Liver - Wind
E225. Liver - Wind with ascending liver Yang
E226. Liver - Wind with blood anemic
E227. Liver - Wind with extreme heat
E228. Lung - Qi deficiency
E229. Lung - Mucus-moisture in the lungs
E230. Lung - Mucus-heat in the lungs
E231. Lung - Mucus-cold in the lungs
E232. Lung - Dryness of the lungs
E233. Lung - Wind-heat attacks the lungs
E234. Lung - Wind-cold affects the lungs
E235. Lung - Yin deficiency
E236. Stomach - Bloodstagnation
E237. Stomach - Fire
E238. Stomach - Cold with liquid
E239. Stomach - Nutrition stagnation
E240. Stomach - Qi deficiency
E241. Stomach - Rebellious Qi
E242. Stomach - Yin Emptiness
E243. Spleen - Heat and moisture attack the spleen
E244. Spleen - Coldness and moisture affects the spleen
E245. Spleen - Qi deficiency
E246. Spleen - Qi deficiency + Declining spleen Qi
E247. Spleen - Qi deficiency + spleen does not control the blood
E248. Spleen - Yang deficiency
E249. Kidney - Heart and kidney no longer communicate
E250. Kidney - Jing deficiency
E251. Kidney - Kidneys cannot receive the Qi
E252. Kidney - Qi is not stable
E253. Kidney - Yang deficiency
E254. Kidney - Yin deficiency

For further information visit di-book.com.